MW01265322

George Caleb Bingham

Frontier Artist, Missouri Politician

Greg Olson

Truman State University Press
Kirksville, Missouri

Copyright © 2017 Truman State University Press, Kirksville, Missouri, 63501
All rights reserved
tsup.truman.edu

Cover art: George Caleb Bingham, *Self-Portrait*. oil on canvas, c. 1877; and Van Gogh's palette and tubes of paint, photo by Dennis Jarvis.

Cover design: Teresa Wheeler

Library of Congress Cataloging-in-Publication Data

Names: Olson, Greg, 1959- author.
Title: George Caleb Bingham : frontier artist, Missouri politician / Greg Olson.
Description: Kirksville, Missouri : Truman State University Press, 2017. |
  Series: Notable Missourians | Includes bibliographical references and
  index. | Description based on print version record and CIP data provided
  by publisher; resource not viewed.
Identifiers: LCCN 2017010555 (print) | LCCN 2017020815 (ebook) | ISBN
  9781612482071 | ISBN 9781612482064 (library binding : alkaline paper)
Subjects: LCSH: Bingham, George Caleb, 1811-1879—Juvenile literature. | Painters—
  United States—Biography—Juvenile literature. | Painters—Missouri—Biography—
  Juvenile literature. | Politicians—Missouri—Biography—Juvenile literature. |
  Legislators—Missouri—Biography—Juvenile literature. | Frontier and pioneer life—
  West (U.S.)—Juvenile literature. | Frontier and pioneer life in art—Juvenile literature.
  | Missouri—Biography—Juvenile literature.
Classification: LCC ND237.B59 (ebook) | LCC ND237.B59 O47 2017 (print) | DDC
  759.13 [B] –dc23
LC record available at https://lccn.loc.gov/2017010555

The paper in this publication meets or exceeds the minimum requirements of the American National Standard for Information Sciences—Permanence of Paper for Printed Library Materials, ANSI Z39.48–1992.

Contents

Introduction

When George Caleb Bingham was a boy, Missouri was on the western edge of the American frontier. As George was growing up, most settlers were busy trying to carve out a living in the new territory. Few people had time to write novels, compose music, or make art. But George was different. For as long as he could remember, he had wanted to be a painter. Because artists and art teachers were rare on the frontier, George learned what he could from artists who crossed his path. But for the most part, he taught himself to draw and paint.

From the very beginning, the young artist painted the people and scenery that were around him and the events he experienced. He began as a portrait painter, making likenesses of friends and neighbors who could afford to pay him for his work. Soon George was painting scenes of regular people doing the things they did every day. He painted pictures of riverboat men, fur trappers, small-town politicians, and farmers, and his paintings hung in galleries and museums all over Europe and the United States. By painting the subjects he knew well, George Bingham captured the details of life in Missouri like no other artist had before him. 🎨

Chapter 1

A Boy on the Frontier

The first time he laid eyes on the Missouri River town of Franklin, Missouri, George Caleb Bingham was eight years old. The year was 1819 and Missouri was still a territory, not yet a state. The town had been founded and named for Benjamin Franklin just three years earlier. It already had a population of one thousand people, and more wagonloads and boatloads of new arrivals like George and his family were coming into town every day. Franklin's riverfront was a hive of activity. Riverboat men, traders, slaves, Native Americans, and soldiers mingled among rafts, keelboats, and even steamboats, which were traveling the river for the first time in 1819. Some families stopped in Franklin for supplies before traveling farther west on the river. Others traveled west on the Boonslick Road, which was named after the nearby salt works operated by Daniel Boone's sons. Still others, like the Binghams, stayed to try to make a new life in Franklin and the surrounding area.

Salt was important before refrigeration because it was used to keep meat from spoiling and to preserve vegetables. Salt can be made by collecting brine (salt water) and boiling it until the water evaporates and only the salt is left. At Boone's Lick, it took about 300 gallons of brine to make a bushel of salt.

For the Bingham family, Franklin must have been a welcome sight. George, along with his parents, grandfather, five brothers and sisters, and seven slaves, had just made the 850-mile trip from their home in Augusta County, Virginia. George had been born there in 1811. In Virginia, George's parents, Henry Vest Bingham and Mary Amend Bingham, had been forced to sell their mill and more than 1,000 acres of land to pay off a loan. The Binghams had helped a friend by co-signing a loan with him, and when their friend died suddenly, they had to pay back the money.

After losing their mill and their land, the Binghams needed a new home where they could start over. Henry Bingham traveled to Missouri with neighbors in 1818 to see what the new territory had to offer. Stopping in St. Louis, he was impressed with the good farmland he saw. He heard about land farther west on the Missouri

Though many people traveled by river, many still traveled by land, using covered wagons that were pulled by horses or oxen.

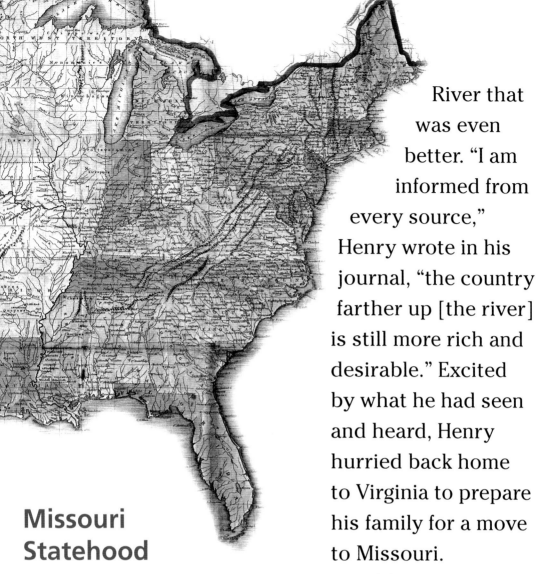

River that was even better. "I am informed from every source," Henry wrote in his journal, "the country farther up [the river] is still more rich and desirable." Excited by what he had seen and heard, Henry hurried back home to Virginia to prepare his family for a move to Missouri.

The Binghams quickly adjusted to their new home and for four years, they enjoyed a happy life. Henry bought an inn, which he named the Square and Compass. He also bought a cigar

Missouri Statehood

Missouri became part of the United States when the country bought the Louisiana Purchase from France in 1803. When Missouri became a state in 1821, it was the farthest west of all the American states. In 1845, Texas entered the Union and replaced Missouri as the country's westernmost state.

factory and a tobacco farm. Henry became an important member of the Franklin community. He served as a justice of the peace and a judge of the county court. But the family's good luck came to a sudden end when Henry died in 1823. George was only twelve years old, and he had five younger brothers and sisters. Again the family had to pay off debts. Mary and her family had to sell everything they owned. Without her husband's income, Mary had to find a way to earn a living. She opened a school for girls in Franklin. She later moved the school to the nearby town of Arrow Rock.

Mary was only able to keep the tobacco farm after the Masonic Lodge Henry had belonged to raised money to help with the payment. The family moved to the farm, which was near Arrow Rock. With the help of George's uncle, John Bingham, and his family, Mary and her children started over yet again. By this time, George was sixteen years old. His uncle John wanted George to find a useful trade to help support his mother. But by that time, George knew that he wanted to be an artist.

George discovered at an early age that he liked to draw. The family said that even as a small boy, George drew pictures on the side of the barn and other buildings on their farm. When George was nine years old, he had a rare chance to watch a real artist at work. In 1820, the American artist Chester Harding stayed at George's father's inn for several days. Harding was in Missouri to paint a picture of the famous frontierman Daniel Boone, who was living near the Missouri River between Franklin and St. Louis. During his stay at the inn, Harding set up a studio. For the first time in his life, George got to watch a real artist at work. It was one of the most important events of his childhood.

Mary encouraged her son's interest in art and allowed him

Daniel Boone was famous even during his lifetime. Accounts of his adventures were popular in both Europe and America. In 1799, Daniel Boone led a group of families from Kentucky to what is now Missouri, where they settled in the St. Louis area. At the time, the region was part of Spanish territory. This painting by Chester Harding is the only life portrait of Daniel Boone. It was painted just weeks before his death in 1820.

to spend time drawing as long as he also helped out on the farm and at the school. Finding paper, art materials, and talented teachers on the frontier was hard. George got some help from one of the teachers at his mother's school, Mattie Wood. Even so, most of what the young artist learned, he learned on his own.

When George was seventeen, he moved to Boonville, Missouri, where he apprenticed with Reverend Justinian Williams, a cabinetmaker and Methodist minister. For four years, George learned to make furniture and spent hours talking about with Reverend Williams about the Bible and religion. During these years, George also learned to paint signs and he met Chester Harding one more time. Harding told George that he might be able to make a living

An apprentice is a young person who learns a certain trade by working for a master craftsman in exchange for being taught the craft. The apprentice usually lives with the master craftsman's family.

as a portrait painter. If a person wanted a picture of themselves or their family, they had to hire an artist to paint a portrait. Harding was also a portrait painter and said there were plenty of people who could afford the price of a portrait. He encouraged George to travel to big city museums and study the art of the famous artists of Europe. George decided to take Harding's advice. He ended his apprenticeship with Reverend Williams and struck out on his own. 🎨

In the early 1800s, painting supplies were hard to transport. Artists had to carry their paints in glass bottles that could break or animal bladders that could leak. In 1841, tin tubes were invented to hold premixed oil paints.

Chapter 2

The Young Portrait Painter

George probably painted his first portraits in Arrow Rock while he was in his early twenties. Among his first subjects were his neighbors Dr. John Sappington and his wife, Jane Breathitt Sappington. Chester Harding had been right when he told George there were many people who could afford to have their portrait painted. But George soon learned that he would have to travel to larger towns and cities to find enough paying customers to earn a living. Within a year, the young artist was on the road, painting portraits in the Missouri towns of Columbia, St. Louis, Liberty, and Boonville.

Travel in the 1830s was difficult and slow. It could take three weeks to get from Missouri to New York City. Railroads had not yet reached Missouri, so the fastest way to travel in George's time was by river. By the 1830s, steamboats had made travel on the Missouri River faster, but steamboats could get stuck on a sandbar or break down, and they could not travel in the winter when rivers were frozen. On land, people traveled on foot, by horse, or by wagon and

Before photography, someone who wanted a portrait had to have enough money to pay a painter, so portraits were usually of people in the middle class or above, and they dressed in their best clothes. Genre paintings became popular because they portrayed people of all classes, backgrounds, and trades.

stagecoach. Roads were often just ruts in the grass that were dusty when it was dry and muddy when it rained. There were few road signs to show the way and it was easy to get lost.

While he was traveling, George came down with smallpox. The disease was common in those days and was very serious. While he was sick, George was not able to work for several weeks. When he did recover, George had scars on his face that never went away. The disease also caused him to lose all of his hair. For the rest of his life, he had to wear a wig.

The wig led to some funny and awkward

Until recently, cameras used film to create pictures. During the early years of photography, the subject had to stay very still for a long time because it took a long time for the image to transfer onto the film.

moments over the years. Once George was staying with his friend James Rollins in Columbia. James's young son, Curtis, got a surprise he would never forget when George took off his wig at night and exposed his "great white dome" of a bald head.

When George was in his sixties, a waitress accidentally snagged his wig with a button on her sleeve. Before she realized what had happened, she had pulled George's wig off of his head. The waitress and George's wife were both very upset, but George made a joke about it. He told the waitress that since his own hair would not stay on his head, he did not expect someone else's hair to stay there either.

While he was painting portraits in Columbia in 1834, George met James Sidney Rollins. James was a lawyer and politician who was active in the Whig Party. Rollins is sometimes called the father of the University of Missouri because of the important role he played in making sure Columbia became the home of the new school in 1839. The two men became life-long friends. Over the years, James became one of George's biggest supporters. He helped the artist by lending him money and introducing him to important people in Missouri and Washington DC. With James's encouragement, George also became active in politics.

George Caleb Bingham painted a portrait of his wife, Sarah, and their son, Newton, in 1841 when Newton was four years old.

It was a passion that stayed with him all of his life. Even with all of his traveling, George found time to fall in love. In April 1836, when he was twenty-four years old, George married sixteen-year-old Sarah Elizabeth Hutchison. Sarah was from Franklin and the pair was married in Boonville. Life for the young couple was a challenge because George moved so often. Soon after their wedding, the newlyweds left Missouri for Natchez, Mississippi. They lived there for several months while George painted portraits. Sarah gave birth to the couple's first child, Isaac Newton Bingham, in Natchez in March 1837.

Soon George and Sarah returned to Arrow Rock with their new baby. The artist bought land there and built a studio. The family had barely settled into their new home when George left his wife and son with relatives in order to travel once more. Remembering the artist Harding's advice, George toured the eastern United States to study the paintings of the great masters. The trip was important because the only way George could see great works of art was to visit them in person. There were no major art museums in Missouri at that time and art books did not yet contain color photographs of paintings.

George and Sarah Bingham built a house in 1837 after they returned to Arrow Rock from a long stay in Natchez, Mississippi. The Binghams lived in this house off and on during the 1840s. The house has been restored and still stands today as a National Historic Landmark.

Genre Painting

"Genre" means "type" or "category." The word is often used to define a style of music, like country, jazz, or classical, or a type of story, like science fiction, mystery, or historical fiction. Genre painting is a style of art that shows scenes of common people and their everyday life. Even though genre paintings show everyday scenes, the artists often had to use their imagination to come up with the specific details of the scenes and the people.

George spent time studying at the Pennsylvania Academy of Fine Art in Philadelphia, where Chester Harding lived. He also traveled to New York and Baltimore. George visited art galleries, museums, and bookstores. The trip exposed the self-taught artist to works of art by some of the best artists from Europe and America. By looking at the work of the masters, George could see how they used color, light, and shadows, and where they placed figures on the canvas. This gave George many new ideas for his own work.

Many of the paintings George saw were of gods and goddesses, kings and queens, and aristocrats and famous people. Many paintings showed important historic events, stories from mythology, or religious scenes. But George discovered that a few artists were painting scenes from everyday life and showing everyday people. These popular "genre" paintings excited George greatly because the people he saw in them looked like the regular people he knew in Missouri. George returned to Arrow Rock with plaster casts of famous sculptures and several printed copies of paintings that he could use for further study. He also brought home a new desire to make genre paintings about everyday life in Missouri. 🎨

Chapter 3

Art and Politics

While George was away in Philadelphia, Sarah gave birth to their second son, who they named Nathaniel. At that time, medical science was not very advanced, and there were few doctors on the frontier. It was not uncommon for children to die from illnesses that are easy to cure today. Nathaniel became sick and soon died. George and Sarah were badly shaken by their loss, but they took comfort in the fact that their first son, Newton, was healthy.

George continued to travel, painting portraits in towns like St. Louis, Fayette, and Glasgow. Even though he wanted to paint pictures that showed everyday life in Missouri, those paintings presented the artist with new challenges. Genre paintings often took more time to paint than portraits and they were usually harder to sell. People were interested in buying a portrait of someone important to them, but few people wanted to buy pictures of common riverboat men, fur traders, farmers, or other people they did not know. Although George is today best known for his genre paintings, for most of his career, portraits were his main source of income.

In 1840, George and his friend James Rollins became involved in the upcoming presidential election. They wanted the Whig candidate, William Henry Harrison, to win. That summer, the meeting of Missouri Whigs was held in the river town of Rocheport, not far from Boonville. In late May, George was hard at work painting banners for the meeting. In a letter to

Using vaccines was not a common practice in the 1800s, so it was not unusual for children to die of a disease that today we don't consider to be very dangerous. Today, those same diseases can be prevented with vaccinations.

23

his friend Thomas Miller, George wrote that he wanted the banners to "be worthy of the occasion." The artist was afraid that he would have to work right up to the day of the meeting to finish them. Not only did George make signs for the meeting, he and his friend James both made speeches in support of their candidate. George learned that he had a gift for public speaking. It was a talent that would serve him well later in his life.

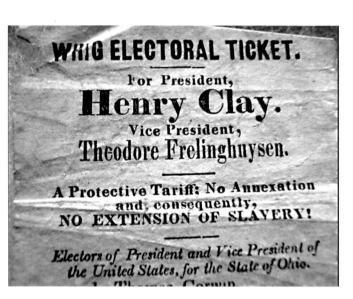

Henry Clay ran for president three times between 1824 and 1844, but he never won. He helped found the Whig Party in the 1830s.

In November, Harrison won the presidential election and George moved his family to Washington DC the following month. With a Whig president about to move into the White House, George hoped that his ties with the party would help him find more work as an artist. Life in the capital city would also help George stay up to date on the latest political events.

While he was in Washington, George stayed in touch with his friends in Missouri. He wrote to his friend James, who by now was a Missouri state representative, asking if he would try to use his power to help George get paid to paint portraits of George Washington and Thomas Jefferson for the state's new capitol building in Jefferson City. George would get that job, but not until years later, after he moved back to Missouri.

In the meantime, George set up a studio in an unused room in the U.S. Capitol, which was still being built. He did find work painting portraits, including one of a former president.

John Quincy Adams became the sixth president of the United States after being elected in 1824. After his term as president, he was a member of the House of Representatives for seventeen years.

Early American Political Parties

The United States' first political parties formed in the 1790s. The Federalists were led by Alexander Hamilton and the Democratic-Republicans were led by James Madison and Thomas Jefferson. In 1829, the Democratic-Republican Party split into the Jacksonian Democrats, led by Andrew Jackson, and the Whig Party, led by Henry Clay. The Whig Party lasted until the 1850s.

One day, while George was working in his studio, an elderly man stopped by to look at the artist's work. George did not know the man, but the two began to talk about the Bible and religion. George had learned a lot about the topic while working with Reverend Williams years before in Boonville. The visitor was so impressed with George's knowledge that he told him, "Young man, if you know as much about painting portraits as you do about the Bible, you are an artist and I'll give you a sitting." That man turned out to be John Quincy Adams, the sixth president of the United States.

Soon after moving to Washington, the Binghams suffered both tragedy and joy on the same day. George and Sarah were looking forward to the birth of a new baby. But early in the morning of March 13, 1841, their four year-old son Newton died of croup, a

George Caleb Bingham took *Fur Traders Descending the Missouri* with him on a trip to St. Louis in 1845. Bingham liked to take his paintings on tours so he could sell copies. This genre painting appealed to both people on the frontier and people in eastern states. The settlers liked the painting because it portrayed an everyday scene for them. People in eastern cities liked it because the painting represented the unknown world of the frontier.

respiratory infection. Just twelve hours later, Sarah gave birth to a baby boy, Horace.

After living in the Washington DC area for nearly four years, the family moved back to Boonville in September 1844. George was in his early thirties and had a growing family. A daughter, Clara, was born on March 14, 1845. George was always eager to make

Today, *The Jolly Flatboatmen* is owned by the National Gallery of Art in Washington DC. Because prints of this painting sold so well, Bingham decided to paint two more versions of this scene. However, neither of those versions sold as well as the original version.

money, so he set to work on a plan he thought would make it easier to sell his genre paintings. George sent paintings to the American Art-Union in New York City. The Art-Union had thousands of paying members across the country. It helped artists make a living by using that money to buy paintings. Members of the Art-Union received an engraved print copy of at least one painting each year. Members also had a chance to win an original work of art.

28

In 1845 George sent four paintings to the Art-Union. They bought all four. One of the paintings, *Fur Traders Descending the Missouri*, is now owned by the Metropolitan Museum of Art in New York and is very popular with museum visitors today. The following year, the Art-Union bought George's painting *The Jolly Flatboatmen* and made a print of it. Suddenly, nearly 10,000 copies of George's painting were being sold all over the United States. The print quickly made George one of the best-known artists in America and the painting became the most famous of his works during his lifetime. With this success, the artist entered a new phase of his career as both an artist and a politician. 🎨

Chapter 4

Missouri's Artist

At the age of thirty-five, George worked hard to balance his interest in art with his interest in politics. In 1846, he ran in a election to represent Saline County in the Missouri state legislature. The race was very close and George won the election over Erasmus D. Sappington by just three votes. Sappington challenged the election results. After an investigation, the legislature declared Sappington to be the winner. This made George very angry. In a letter to James Rollins, he complained that he had been cheated. "As soon as I get through with his affair," he wrote, "I intend to strip off my clothes and bury them, scour my body all over with sand and water, put on a clean suit. And keep out of the mire of politics *forever*."

But two years later, George changed his mind and ran against Sappington again. This time he won by enough votes that Sappington could not challenge the result. Just as George was preparing to travel to Jefferson City, Sarah died of tuberculosis. George's mother, Mary, was left to care for Clara, Horace, and a new baby boy named Joseph. But soon Joseph died too, just a few weeks after his mother.

George was heartbroken, but the legislature was ready to meet and he was forced to travel to the state capitol. The mood in the legislature was very tense. The issue of slavery seemed to be dividing

Polling officials wrote election returns to report the number of votes that were cast for each candidate. They also reported the number of votes for or against a plan proposed by the government.

31

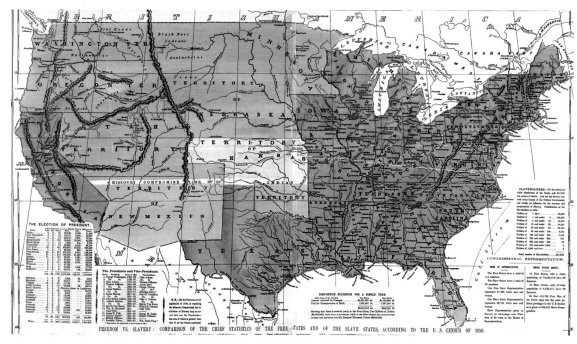

FREEDOM VS. SLAVERY: COMPARISON OF THE CHIEF STATISTICS OF THE FREE STATES AND OF THE SLAVE STATES, ACCORDING TO THE U. S. CENSUS OF 1850.

The Missouri Compromise of 1820 stated that slavery was not allowed in the Louisiana Territory north of a certain line of latitude, except in Missouri. The Supreme Court declared the Missouri Compromise unconstitutional in 1857, stating that Congress did not have the power to forbid slavery in the territories. This map shows the free states in pink, the slave states in gray, and the territories in green.

the state and the nation. Missouri State Senator Claiborne Fox Jackson had introduced a resolution calling for Missouri representatives to Congress in Washington DC to argue that the federal government had no right to control which states could allow slavery and which could not. Jackson and his supporters wanted slavery to be allowed in the new lands in the west that would soon become states. George was sure Jackson's resolutions would tear the country apart, so he came up with his own list of resolutions.

32

George was not against slavery. He had been born in a slave state and his family brought slaves with them when they moved to Missouri from Virginia. In fact, George still owned two slaves in 1850. He did not want to make slavery illegal, but he did not want to allow slavery in new states. Above all, George did not want the United States to split over the issue. He wanted to keep the Union together.

The legislature did not approve George's resolutions and he did not run for re-election in 1850. By then George was remarried, to Eliza K. Thomas, and he was eager to spend more time on his art. George had ideas for a new series of paintings that would show democracy at work in Missouri.

In 1851, he began to work on the first of these paintings, *The County Election*. It took George several months to finish the painting. At four feet wide and three feet high, the painting is very large and includes dozens of figures. While the scene was set in Arrow Rock, George said that *The County Election* could take place in any state in the United State. He wrote that it illustrated "free people and free institutions" of democracy. The painting shows an unruly frontier scene in which men line up to cast their ballots on election day. Some men in the painting are debating.

Art experts believe this painting represents the 1846 election day in Saline County, when Bingham ran against Sappington.

Some men are joking. One man sadly hangs his head. George upset some people by showing one man raising a glass of whiskey. Another man appears to have had so much whiskey that he needs help getting to the ballot box. *The County Election* shows that democracy works, but the people who take part in it are not always perfect or totally noble.

From the beginning, George planned to have engraved copies made of *The County Election*. He remembered how thousands of copies of *The Jolly Flatboatmen* had spread his name across the country. He also hoped to be able to make more money by selling hundreds of prints rather than just one painting. For this reason, he made a copy of the painting in 1852.

He sent the first painting to an engraver who would make a print of it. He took the second painting around the county to try to get people to order print copies.

George painted two more paintings in the series. He finished *Stump Speaking* in 1854 and *The Verdict of the People* in 1855. The paintings show other important parts of the democratic process. *Stump Speaking* shows a candidate making a campaign speech to a group of men and boys. *The Verdict of the People* shows election results being read out to a crowd on the steps of a building that looks like the Boone County Courthouse in Columbia. Like *The County Election*, both of these paintings include dozens of figures in various poses doing different things. George was careful to give each figure he painted its own personality to represent the common people he knew on the frontier. Some believed that he painted both friends and enemies in his genre paintings, but George denied it. Just as he had

Who Could Vote?

The County Election shows only white men casting their votes, because in 1852 blacks and women could not vote. The 14th Amendment gave blacks the right to vote in 1870. The 19th Amendment gave women the right to vote in 1920.

Today *The Verdict of the People* is owned by the Saint Louis Art Museum. Art experts think that this painting shows the public's reaction when a candidate who supported slavery won an election.

done with *The County Election*, George made two copies of *Stump Speaking* and *The Verdict of the People* so he could have engraved copies made to sell. Because the engraver's shop was in France, George and Eliza and George's daughter, Clara, spent more than two years living in Europe.

At home, American politics were becoming as unruly as the scenes in one of George's paintings. Slavery threatened to tear the country apart and civil war seemed possible. In the coming years, George would face some of the biggest challenges of his artistic and political life. 🎨

Chapter 5

The Civil War

After George returned to the Unites States from Europe, he was as busy as ever. The state legislature finally approved his plan to paint portraits for the State Capitol building and he had many other projects in the works. But in 1861, politics interrupted George's art career once again when the Civil War broke out after Abraham Lincoln was elected president.

In the summer of 1861, the war came to Missouri. Governor Claiborne Fox Jackson wanted Missouri to join the Confederate states. He and other government officials left Jefferson City to set up a

Confederate state capitol in Neosho, Missouri. The federal government declared the offices of those who had gone to Neosho to be vacant, and chose Union supporters to fill the empty offices.

George wanted to help the Union any way he could. When the war started, he joined the army, even though he was almost twice as old as most other soldiers. After he got out of the army, George got a new job. With the help of his friend James Rollins,

After the Missouri state officials who supported the South left the Union in 1861, the new Missouri government began to organize regiments to fight for the Union. By the end of the Civil War there were nearly 450 Missouri regiments fighting for the Union.

George was chosen to fill the vacant office of Missouri state treasurer. In 1862, George and his family, which now included a new baby, James Rollins Bingham, moved to Jefferson City.

George was known for his strong opinions and his quick temper. Sometimes these traits got the best of him. During the Civil War, they led him into a public battle with Union general Thomas Ewing. It was Ewing's job to keep Confederate fighters, known as bushwhackers, from attacking people along the Missouri and Kansas border.

George's trouble with Ewing began when the general took over his mother-in-law's house in Kansas City to use as a jail for women who were charged with helping Confederates. In August 1863, the house collapsed and five women died. George blamed

Bushwackers and Jayhawkers

Missouri was a dangerous place during the Civil War. Men who were not part of any regular army killed many people and caused a lot of damage. Confederate supporters called bushwhackers, or border ruffians, roamed the country in small groups to scare and kill those who supported the Union. They often clashed with groups of Union supporters known as jayhawkers.

General Ewing for the damage to his mother-in-law's house and for the deaths of the women.

A few days later, Ewing issued Order No. 11. The general believed that there were so many Confederate supporters in western Missouri, the only way for the Union to keep control of the area was to order everyone who lived in a four-county area along the Kansas border to leave their homes. After the people left, some Union soldiers stole what was left behind and burned many buildings to the ground. The destruction was so great that the area became known as the "burnt-over district." The removal of people and the damage made George so angry that he traveled to face the general and ask him to change his mind. When Ewing refused, George vowed to get even. Some say he told Ewing, "I will make you infamous with pen and brush as far as I am able."

Soon after George's term as state treasurer ended in 1865, he started work on his large painting *Order No. 11* and his promise to get even with Ewing. The painting took George three years to finish. It shows the suffering of a western Missouri family at the hands of a group of Union soldiers. One of the soldiers in the painting was Ewing. George painted two copies of *Order No. 11*, just as he had with his earlier

Order No. 11 did not sell as well as Bingham had hoped. Critics at the time thought that the painting unfairly criticized the Union soldiers and even showed sympathy toward the South.

political paintings. He sent one copy to engravers in Philadelphia to make prints. George used the second copy to sell prints of the painting. While on tour, George talked about the suffering he thought General Ewing had caused the people of Missouri.

By this time, George was nearly sixty years old and his health was growing worse. He still traveled and he was always looking for ways to make money to support his family. In 1869, he became the director of schools in Independence, Missouri. He also worked as Kansas City's police commissioner for a short time. In 1875,

Governor Charles Hardin chose George to be the state's adjutant general. In this job, George was in charge of the state's militias, which are like today's national guard. During these years, George also painted more large portraits for the Missouri State Capitol building.

But tragedy followed George into old age. In 1869, George's son Horace died at the age of twenty-eight. A few years later, George's wife, Eliza, began to suffer from mental illness. In the 1870s, doctors did not know much about mental illnesses, so there was very little they could do to help her. In 1876, Eliza died in the Fulton State Hospital.

In 1877, at the age of sixty-six, George seemed find some happiness. His old friend James Rollins

George Caleb Bingham painted two portraits for the Senate Chamber in the Missouri State Capitol. His portrait of George Washington hung on the left and his portrait

of Henry Clay hung on the right. Both paintings were destroyed when the building burned down in 1911.

MO. SENATE CHAMBER

42

helped George become the University of Missouri's first professor of art. George was also allowed to set up a studio at the university and work there. The following year, he married his third wife, Martha Livingston Lykins. She was the widow of Johnston Lykins, a friend of George's who had once been the mayor of Kansas City. She was also a Southern supporter who had been forced to leave her home by Ewing's Order No. 11 during the Civil War.

But George's health continued to get worse. He died on July 7, 1879, at the age of sixty-eight. His widow had him buried near her first husband in Union Cemetery in Kansas City. 🎨

Even during his lifetime, George Caleb Bingham was known as "the Missouri Artist." In 2010 a bust of Bingham was put in the Hall of Famous Missourians at the State Capitol to honor his art and his contribution to Missouri history.

An Artist for Missouri and for America

George Caleb Bingham painted the people, places, and events that he knew and experienced in everyday life around him. Because he lived at a time when photography was not common, his work is an important record of life on the American frontier. Even though most of George's paintings show Missouri scenes, many people think of George Caleb Bingham as a painter of all America, not just Missouri.

George Caleb Bingham's genre paintings are still popular today because they show how a new nation worked to create itself and show what life was like for everyday people. His political paintings show democracy in action in small western towns. His river scenes show steamboats, flatboats, and rivermen moving goods across this huge continent. To many, the art of George Caleb Bingham represents the birth of the United States. 🎨

Timeline

March 20, 1811: George Caleb Bingham is born in Augusta County, Virginia.

1819: Eight-year-old George Bingham moves to Franklin, Missouri, with his family and their slaves.

1820: The American painter Chester Harding stays at the Bingham family's inn, the Square and Compass.

1833: George begins to support himself as a portrait painter.

1836: George marries sixteen-year-old Sarah Elizabeth Hutchison.

1838: George completes *Western Boatman Ashore*, his first known genre painting.

1840: George joins his friend and supporter James Sydney Rollins as a speaker at the state Whig Party meeting in Rocheport, Missouri. George remains active in politics for the rest of his life.

1848: George is elected to the Missouri State Legislature. He serves one two-year term. His wife, Sarah, dies.

1849: George marries Eliza Thomas.

1850: George begins the first of his three most famous political paintings. He completes *The County Election* in 1852, *Stump Speaking* in 1853, and *The Verdict of the People* in 1855.

1861: The Civil War begins; George joins the army.

1862: Governor Hamilton Gamble appoints George to the office of Missouri State Treasurer.

1865: The Civil War ends. George begins work on *Order No. 11*, which he finishes three years later.

1875: Governor Charles Hardin appoints George to be Missouri's adjutant-general.

1876: George's second wife, Eliza, dies.

1877: George becomes the University of Missouri's first professor of art.

1878: George marries Martha Livingston Lykins.

July 7, 1879: George dies in Kansas City at the age of sixty-eight.

For Further Reading

For Young Readers

Bliss, John. *Pioneers to the West*. Chicago: Raintree, 2012.

Collier, Christopher, and James Lincoln Collier. *Slavery and the Coming of the Civil War, 1831–1861*. New York: Benchmark Books, 2000.

Galford, Ellen. *The Trail West: Exploring History through Art*. Minnetonka, MN: Two-Can Publishing, 2004.

Hughes, Pat. *Guerrilla Season*. New York: Farrar, Straus, and Giroux, 2003.

Raczka, Bob. *No One Saw: Ordinary Things through the Eyes of an Artist*. Brookfield, CT: Millbrook Press, 2002.

Raczka, Bob. *Unlikely Pairs: Fun with Famous Works of Art*. Minneapolis, MN: Millbrook Press, 2006.

Roop, Peter, and Connie Roop. *River Roads West: America's First Highways*. Honesdale, PA: Calkins Creek, 2007.

Websites

High Museum of Art (Atlanta). *American Encounters: Genre Paintings and Everyday Life*. https://www.high.org/Art/Exhibitions/American-Encounters.aspx

Kline, Fred R. *George Caleb Bingham: Artist of Missouri and the American Frontier*. http://www.georgecalebbingham.org/bio.htm [includes links to show Bingham's paintings].

Metropolitan Museum. *Heilbrunn Timeline of Art History: American Scenes of Everyday Life, 1840–1910*. http://www.metmuseum.org/toah/hd/scen/hd_scen.htm

Metropolitan Museum. *Heilbrunn Timeline of Art History: Fur*

Traders Descending the Missouri. http://www.metmuseum.org/toah/works-of-art/33.61/

National Park Service: CWSAC Battle Summaries [Civil War battles sites in Missouri]. https://www.nps.gov/abpp/battles/MOmap.htm

Smithsonian Institution. *Nineteenth-Century Art: The Hudson River School and the Lure of the West.* http://americanart.si.edu/collections/highlights/19th/

State Historical Society of Missouri. *Guide to American Civil War in Missouri.* http://shsmo.org/research/guides/civil-war/images/

Sources

Bloch, E. Maurice. *The Paintings of George Caleb Bingham: A Catalogue Raisonné.* Columbia: University of Missouri Press, 1986.

Christ-Janer, Albert. *George Caleb Bingham: Frontier Painter of Missouri.* New York: H. N. Abrams, 1975.

Gentzler, Lynn Wolf, ed. *"But I Forgot That I am a Painter and Not a Politician:" The Letters of George Caleb Bingham.* Columbia: State Historical Society of Missouri, 2011.

Grissom, Daniel M. "Personal Recollections of Distinguished Missourians: George Caleb Bingham." *Missouri Historical Review* 21 (October 1926): 56–58.

Nagel, Paul C. *George Caleb Bingham: Missouri's Famed Painter and Forgotten Politician.* Columbia: University of Missouri Press, 2005.

Rollins, C. B. "Some Recollections of George Caleb Bingham." *Missouri Historical Review* 40 (October 1945): 463–83.

Windell, Marie George, ed. "The Road West in 1818, The Diary of Henry Vest Bingham: Part 1." *Missouri Historical Review* 20 (July 1926): 21–54.

Index

Image Credits